Appreciative Team Building

Appreciative Team Building

Positive Questions to Bring Out the Best of Your Team

Diana Whitney,
Amanda Trosten-Bloom,
Jay Cherney and Ron Fry

iUniverse, Inc.
New York Lincoln Shanghai

Appreciative Team Building
Positive Questions to Bring Out the Best of Your Team

iUniverse, Inc.

For information address:
iUniverse, Inc.
2021 Pine Lake Road, Suite 100
Lincoln, NE 68512
www.iuniverse.com

ISBN: 0-595-33503-9

Printed in the United States of America

Contents

Section 1:
Introduction

We all live amidst the wonder and potential of teams and teamwork. Nearly every significant accomplishment by human systems today comes from the cooperation, positive energy and learning that result from a real team effort. Everywhere we turn, teamwork is a primary vehicle through which we advance our lives and careers. From families to communities, athletic teams to task forces, volunteer committees to rapid deployment teams, blue ribbon panels to indigenous tribes, boards of directors to manufacturing cells, autonomous work groups to personal growth groups—teams and teamwork propel progress.

While the concept of *teams* is arguably a western invention and a legacy of the industrial age, indigenous cultures for time immemorial have engaged groups of people for common purposes, encouraging them to cooperate across and learn through their members' differences and uniqueness. In modern organizations, no matter the cultural context, teams are the main integrating structure, or vehicle, to bring about shared meaning, innovation and collaboration across multi-functional and multiple stakeholder interests.

In such a team-oriented context, why introduce another book on the subject? So many books and guides already fill the team sections of the management shelves of most noteworthy bookstores and their websites. They are full of prescriptions about how to achieve trust, cohesion, authentic exchange, shared goals and the like. Yet the books keep coming, suggesting that there is still a yearning for something that enables people to relate to their specific team in a particular context, to help them value the exceptionality of their situation. Our intent in this book is not to tell readers how they should go about the act of teaming, what goals to set or what roles to define. Rather, our purpose here is to help foster understanding of why teams work when they do. It is to nurture an ongoing curiosity that, when acted upon, will give life to a team, feeding its capacity to grow and to be effective.

This book is a catalogue of questions that will begin conversations among team members. These conversations, in turn, will enable them to discover the keys to both past successes and future possibilities. The aim of this book is to help readers steer their teams' conversations in such a way as to generate even more cohesiveness, cooperation, shared meaning, creativity and productivity.

The Power of Questions

Those who are familiar with Appreciative Inquiry (AI) have already recognized our emphasis on questions over answers. With the topics of teams and effective teamwork, sensitivity to the questions we ask is especially relevant. Consider a common workplace conversation. When asked, "What do you think about our team meetings?" we might reply, "We have way too many. They're disorganized, and they distract us from the 'real' work that needs to get done." Yet when asked, "Would our organization benefit from better teamwork?" most of us would respond with a resounding *yes*. It is as if we simultaneously carry very high hopes for what teams can accomplish and histories that are filled with missed or less than fulfilled opportunities. The deficit discourse that pervades many of our social institutions also affects our memories and conversations about past team experiences. Appreciative Inquiry is a well-documented, strength-based method to shift this conversation and reflection toward generative stories of moments when teams were at their very best.[1] These stories serve as the basis for an analysis and *discovery* of the core success factors that already reside in a team's repertoire. With these discoveries in hand, conversations shift to *dreaming* about an ideal future and then *designing* and implementing ways to continuously move toward that ideal *destiny*.

This positive, collaborative and innovative process begins with intentionally different questions than we typically ask. It is a major departure from the *modus operandi* in most organizations, in which we take a group of well intentioned, smart people, put them in a team and throw some complex organizational issue at them. Indeed, we believe that far too many organizations take this approach and settle for the resulting mediocrity. Whatever the team can agree on is received as a success. In fact, just getting any agreement becomes the shared goal—an unfortunate surrogate for the more appropriate goal of breakthrough thinking or real partnership across functional boundaries or quantum leaps in efficiencies. Without careful attention, teams tend to drift into a pattern of conversation that describes what they don't want: wasteful meetings, conflicts that breed defensiveness and personal attacks, hidden agendas and poor listening that result in lack of progress and mutual distrust. Even if these pitfalls are recognized as activities to prevent, they occupy an inordinate amount of the team's time and foster images of what might go wrong, instead of what can go right.

Even in training programs to help teams develop effectively, the most popular models today shape participants to expect and welcome *storming* as a necessary phase of a good team's development. The very idea that in order to get better at teamwork, we *must* engage in some special form of fighting or arguing with one another is a reason people partly dread being assigned to new teams or projects. The language itself shapes powerful, often self-fulfilling prophecies. And as if this were not enough, serious students and researchers of team dynamics have given us deficit-based theories about anxiety provoking settings in which our individual self-efficacy is at odds with the desire to belong.[2] Such paradoxes can only be suffered through, as there are often no *win-win* outcomes.[3]

In working with AI, our colleagues and we have consistently found that questions are fateful; that they, more than anything else, can alter a conversation and choreograph a process to one end or another. The questions in this book offer a way to (re)shape conversations and alter trajectories in teams so that members are more likely to eagerly anticipate coming together and to interact with words and stories that create positive images about past and future teamwork.

Why Alter the Conversation in Teams?

Many team building and team improvement processes are implemented with an eye towards making people happier or more productive. For some, these are good enough reasons for changing how people relate to and work with one another. People should be able to enjoy work and those they work with—and yes, satisfaction is related to productivity. But we believe in shifting conversations in teams for another reason. We believe that strength-based, affirmative, generative and hope-full conversations add value both to the bottom line and to individual team members.

Consider the recent, groundbreaking research by Marcial Losada and Emily Heaphy.[4] They took 60 business teams and ranked them in terms of performance, as measured by profit and loss statements, customer satisfaction surveys and 360 reviews by superiors, peers and subordinates to the teams. After grouping the High, Medium and Low performing teams, they analyzed three aspects of the teams' conversations: positivity vs. negativity (P:N), inquiry vs. advocacy (I:A) and other vs. self comments (O:S). The results were provocative, to say the least.

- High performing teams had an average P:N ratio of 5.8 to 1 and were balanced (1:1) in I:A and O:S.

- Medium performing teams were only slightly more positive than negative (P:N = 1.8 to 1) and slightly weighted towards both advocacy (2:3) and self oriented conversation (2:3).

- Low performing teams were highly negative (P:N = 1 to 20), more advocacy oriented (I:A = 1 to 3), and very self oriented in their interactions (O:S = 1 to 30).

Further, the study demonstrated that the P:N ration was the key driver in influencing the other two ratios. In other words, both a healthy 1:1 balance in internal focus on team deliberation and external environmental scanning, and a healthy 1:1 balance of questioning each other to understand and asserting one's opinions and positions, *resulted from* a disproportionate emphasis on positivity over negativity. The positivity in the high performing teams created expansive emotional spaces that revealed a variety of possible actions. The negativity in the other teams created restricted emotional spaces that closed possibilities for action. This supports the work of Fredrickson[5] that shows how positive emotions broaden thought-action repertoires and build durable physical, intellectual and social resources.

So transforming the day-to-day interactions in teams to be more positive than negative is a means to achieving a productive balance between the team's focus on itself and its environment, between seeking understanding and asserting authentic beliefs and opinions. This shift in the pattern of discourse, in turn, leads to measurable success and value added for the organization.

The unconditionally affirmative questions offered in this book can catalyze this transformation. They will immediately alter a team's discourse toward the decidedly positive and add inquiry and concern-for-the-other to the mix during important team conversations.

Dimensions That Influence Team Effectiveness

The questions in this book will stimulate a discovery process that surfaces strengths and best practices that members have experienced in their own and other teams. These factors and ideas then provide the basis for dreaming or imaging an ideal future, together with specific practices to move the team toward those ideals. Each question will generate content or data about key dimensions—any of which have been shown to accompany effective teams in any situation.[6]

- **Clear and shared goals or purpose.** What is the team to accomplish? Why are its members interdependent? What would be indicators of success? What makes this team's work most meaningful to each member?

- **Clear and shared roles/responsibilities.** What important part does each member play? What helps members live up to one another's highest expectations? How do people help each other excel beyond their expectations? How can role conflict become an opportunity for learning and development?

- **Supportive and empowering relationships.** How do people interact, to ensure that everyone learns and grows with every task they take on? How do they ensure that everyone experiences being a necessary and exceptional part of the end result? How does mutual respect and appreciation continue to grow?

- **Clear and shared procedures.** How do members communicate with one another so that everyone has the information needed to perform at the highest individual level? How are meetings conducted so that the time spent is most meaningful to everyone? How do people make important decisions so that everyone is committed to seeing them through?

- **Nurturing and challenging leadership.** How do formal leaders engage people? For what purpose? How is leadership distributed across the organization? How do people leverage their power and influence in service of the organization and its people?

- **Evolving energy and spirit.** How does the team regenerate itself? What rituals do people observe? How do members of the team celebrate success and mark rites of passage?

- **Productivity and performance.** What are team members' connections to the larger organizations they serve? What is the team's *bottom line* contribution? How does work get done? What quality standards does the team hold for itself, and how are those standards implemented?

- **Complete, purposeful and uplifting communication.** Who talks to whom? About what? How? What systems and structures are in place to foster people's connection to the whole and to one another?

In their book *The Wisdom of Teams,* Katzenbach and Smith demonstrate that high performance teams discipline themselves to stop and *inquire* about goals, roles, relationships and procedures on a regular basis in order to avoid confusion or lack of agreement in any area.[7] We suggest that this regular, disciplined inquiry should also cover the topics of energy and spirit, productivity and performance, and communication. Though answers to the questions will vary, the issues to be raised up for appreciation and inquiry are constant. The questions in this book are designed to guide your team into these crucial areas of inquiry—repeatedly. Never assume, for example, that team goals are clear and agreed to by everyone—even when they have been determined and declared the month before with total consent from all. Effective teams revisit these topic areas time and time again, while less effective teams do not.

Start with the Best Team

The early stages of any team effort are fateful. People bring some sense of their prior experiences to the present situation, whether they know their new team members or not. These notions then shape their early actions and reactions. Our colleague Gervase Bushe has used appreciative inquiry in many start-up teams. His "Best Team Intervention" simply, but powerfully, asks the new members to recall stories of exceptional team experiences or moments in previous teams when they discovered something meaningful about themselves, and so on.[8] After sharing their stories, the new team members then work on sifting out the key practices or underlying norms for team operation from the stories that they would most like to see in this new team. Finally, they make specific plans and promises to work in ways to achieve those aspirations.

When compared with other forms of more traditional team building, this approach contributes to higher team effectiveness and cohesion.[9] Referring to these early team moments as a "pre-identity" stage, Bushe asserts that appreciative inquiry is particularly suited and valuable at this point because it transforms possible fear or worry about what could go wrong into confident and practical hope for what might be.

Start Now

The questions, processes and suggestions in this book are offered as food for thought, sampling and experimenting. Adapt them—but by all means try them. Now is the time to shift the conversation in your team more toward the positive; more toward a search for practices that work best for you. Now is the best time to revisit past team experiences that were truly wondrous and valuable to everyone concerned—to remember and understand those things that help teams be the best they can be—in order to build an even better team for the future.

In Section 2 you will find ten suggestions on how to use these and other positive questions to build high performance teams. In Section 3, we have provided you with 48 positive questions, organized by six different subject areas: purpose and goals, roles and responsibilities, procedures, relationships, leadership, energy and spirit, productivity and performance and communication.

We offer Section 4 with some humility. It contains guidelines for a team building process: an Appreciative Inquiry into positive team development. This step-by-step process can be self-facilitated (using the skeleton interview guide provided in Section 5) or guided, depending on the team's needs. Either way, it will enhance the team's capacity through disciplined conversation and study of what works. Finally, Section 6 is a call to action, together with a catalogue of additional resources for those who are attracted to this way of working.

The possibilities to be explored using the questions in this book can be summarized this way: start your next committee or team meeting with an unconditional positive question about what has transpired since the last meeting, listen to the stories that come out, and then marvel at how differently the group approaches the meeting agenda than if they had simply started right into it, as they usually do.

Section 2:
Ten Ways to Use Positive Questions to Build High Performance Teams

Talent wins games, but teamwork wins championships.

—Michael Jordan

1. Selecting Team Members

Some people are natural team players. Others have acquired team skills and know how to cooperate, keep lines of communication open, and share responsibilities and results. These are the kinds of people you want on your team—people with the inclination and skills to be team players.

One of the best ways to discover team players is with positive questions. Select two or three of the questions in this book and use them as part of your selection interview. When you ask these questions, listen attentively. Does the person you are interviewing have experience as part of a successful team? Can she describe what made the team successful? Does he know what he contributed to the team's success, so that he can do it again? Are her skills and strengths attributes you need to make your team successful? By asking positive questions you will gain information and understanding needed to select the right people for your team.

2. Aligning the Strengths of Team Members

High performance teams optimize the strengths of their members. They take time to learn about each team member's interests, skills, strengths, hopes and dreams. They optimize and align strengths toward the vision, purpose and goals of the team.

The questions in this book can help you identify the strengths, hopes and dreams of your team members. Once you discover and create a profile of team members' strengths you can assign roles and responsibilities that play to their strengths. To create a team strength profile, select a few questions from this book (like "Mining Your Assortment of Winning Styles and Temperaments" or "Strengths Working in Synergy") and create an interview guide. Divide your team into pairs and have partners interview one another. Once the interviews are done, hold a team meeting to discuss what you learned in the interviews. Make a chart that shows each team member's team skills, strengths, hopes and desires to learn. This will be your team strength profile. Use it as you go forward to align team members' strengths with team roles and responsibilities.

3. Building Camaraderie and Trust

Both camaraderie and trust depend on team members knowing one another, personally and professionally. Especially in the early stages of team development, people need to take time to meet and learn about one another, to create a foundation of trust and camaraderie right from the start. This foundation serves them well as they get busy, experience the pressure of the task and its timelines, and need to work collaboratively with other people and teams.

To build a foundation of camaraderie and trust, select a question or two from this book on a topic such as trust, team spirit, fun at work or celebrating success. Set aside two to four hours and, as a team, answer the questions. Be sure that everyone answers each question. As you listen to the stories that team members share, make note of common themes and unique highpoints. These will give you clues about how to nurture trust and camaraderie in your team.

After sharing your answers to the questions and discussing the common themes that emerge, you may want to assign people to be responsible for team spirit on a monthly basis. Their task is simply to initiate and facilitate something from the team's list of common themes once in the month—a team heart-to-heart conversation, a team pizza party, a team recognition day. Your team's unique list of ideas will emerge from your discussion of positive questions.

4. Establishing Team Norms

All teams need norms for communication, decision-making and response to timelines, just to name a few. Successful teams explicitly discuss and decide upon their norms. They study other high performing teams and learn what makes them better. They borrow from the best of other teams and from their own prior success experiences to create norms that work for them and their situation.

Use the questions in this book to guide your study of the norms that make other teams successful. Select three to four questions and create an interview guide. Identify some successful teams, and have members of your team conduct interviews with their team members. Pick teams that you currently work with. Pick others that you might need to collaborate with at a later date. You may also choose to interview teams outside of your organization and area of work. For example, if you work in business, you may find it interesting to interview a sports team, an advertising team or a theatrical team to discover their secrets to success.

After you conduct your interviews, gather all your team members and share stories and lessons learned. As you listen to one another, make a list of "Norms for Team Success." After all of you have shared what you've discovered from your interviews, have an open and honest discussion about your team's norms. Finally, decide upon a set of norms (no more than ten) that you all agree to follow.

5. Celebrating Team Successes

All too often—both personally and in teams—we hop from project to project, task to task without celebrating our accomplishments. High performance teams work hard and regularly celebrate their small wins and large, significant successes. Positive questions can help you and your team to recognize and celebrate your progress. In doing so, you will learn what makes you as good as you are. You will enhance team pride in what you do and how you do it, and inspire commitment among team members to the project or work of the team.

You can use positive questions to recognize and celebrate team success informally in a conversation with a colleague or formally by holding a meeting. To stimulate a sense of celebration informally, simply ask your team members, "What about this project, event, or work gives you the greatest sense of pride?" or ask people to talk about who they most appreciate and why. In this way, both individual team members and the team as a whole can be recognized.

Use positive questions to formally celebrate team success. Select a question from this book and ask everyone on the team to use it as a guide to discuss a current project or the overall work of the team. Use a round robin process in which each team member answers the question. After everyone has shared, create a list of accomplishments and identify who contributed to them. Include in this list the stories about the team and some team photos in an internal communication organ—a company newsletter, bulletin board, or intranet site. In this way, others can learn from your team's successes.

6. Clarifying Customer Requirements

High performing teams establish relationships with customers to discover and clarify what those customers want and need. Some teams maintain ongoing relationships with their customers, keeping the door open to dialogue about changing customer requirements. Others make periodic forays into the world of customers with focus groups, surveys and customer interviews. No matter what data collection method you use, positive questions can make a positive difference.

Positive questions can be used in customer focus groups and one-on-one interviews with customers, or they can be designed into customer surveys. Many of the questions in this book can help you to determine customer requirements. Select two or three and ask them of your customers. What you learn in these interviews will help you decide how you can best fulfill their hopes and dreams. Remember, understanding your customer is the key to understanding why your team exists.

7. Aligning Strengths in the Face of Differences

High performance teams thrive on opposition, including differences of opinions, approaches, cultures, ways of thinking and styles of working. They do so by transforming opposition into collaboration. By aligning their strengths in the face of differences, they optimize resources and work efficiently toward their goals. They don't waste time or energy on what doesn't work; instead, they focus on bringing out the best of what works, individually and collectively.

In order to transform opposition into collaboration, team members need to discover and understand their differences. To do this, they must be courageously open to learn what makes them different from one another, and recognize how these differences can serve their team. Only then can they align strengths and work harmoniously toward a common purpose. This is where positive questions come in.

A great way to use positive questions to transform opposition is to ask people to select the one person they think is most different from them and to interview that person using three or four positive questions. As they conduct their interviews, ask them to note those things they discover they have in common with their partner, as well as the ways in which they are different. After they do the interviews, have them share their notes with one another and create a shared list of similarities and differences. Ask them to take the process one step further and imagine and discuss how they might work best together, given those similarities and differences. Entire teams can engage in the same process, creating a list of commonalities and difference among all team members, together with a plan for how the team members can best collaborate.

8. Creating a Project Vision and Goals

"Without a vision the people will perish." This often quoted line from Proverbs is true for both individuals and teams. High performance teams have a compelling vision and clear goals. The vision may be for a specific project, the team as an ongoing work group, or an event or task. Whatever the vision, it must draw both team members and other stakeholders to participate in its realization. And it must point to a set of clear goals necessary for its achievement.

High performance teams take time to articulate their vision and goals. You can do this through a series of positive questions in which team members are asked to envision the organization or community at a time in the future when their purpose has been achieved, or to envision the world a better world because of something they have done. The questions in this book will help. Select one or two (like "When Goals Snap Sharply into Focus") and use them to guide a dialogue about your team's vision for its future. Be bold. Gather many ideas for what is possible, and new ways of realizing these possibilities are sure to emerge.

9. Creating Team Identity and Enhancing Pride

All teams have a unique personality or identity. Some are action oriented, while others are reflective and plan driven. Others are at their best in the face of complex challenges, and still others thrive when maintaining a steady pace of progress. No one identity is better than others. Each has its ups and downs, its strengths and weaknesses. What matters is that team members feel the pride in their team that comes from consciously creating a team identity aligned with their values.

To create a team identity, use positive questions to explore what you and your teammates have valued about other teams they have worked with or observed. You might talk about what you have valued about other teams' decision-making process, leadership, communication, ways of working and relationships with other teams in order to generate a picture of the kind of team that you want to be, one that will give your team a sense of unity and pride.

10. Energizing Team Meetings

One way to create meaningful, engaging team meetings is to involve all team members in the dialogue. When people have an opportunity to participate and share their thoughts, ideas and feelings, they more readily attend to the meeting's agenda and commit to take action. Positive questions are an effective way to get people involved. They create a context for learning and appreciation, and foster a *can do* attitude among team members.

Positive questions can be used to open a meeting. Consider for example this idea: "Before we get into our agenda for today's meeting, let's go around the table and each share what we've done since our last meeting to bring in new business." Beginning meetings with positive questions helps make work sessions more fun, energized and relevant.

Positive questions can also be used to transform the sentiment in a meeting from despair to hope. When conversation deteriorates and team members get stuck going round and round on why something won't work, try a positive question. Ask them, "What is your greatest hope or dream for this situation? What would you like to see happen? If you had a magic wand, what would you wish for in this situation?" Positive questions can pull a team out of the muck and launch it into new and exciting directions.

Section 3:
Positive Questions to Bring Out the Best of Your Team

This section contains 48 positive questions, organized into eight dimensions of team effectiveness and team development:

- Aligning Purpose and Goals
- Clarifying Roles and Responsibilities
- Fostering Supportive and Empowering Relationships
- Creating Clear and Shared Procedures
- Promoting Leadership
- Elevating Energy and Spirit
- Advancing Productivity and Performance
- Stimulating Purposeful and Uplifting Communication

Inquiry into any one of these areas will elevate your team's consciousness and effectiveness in ways that are crucial to high performance. Periodic inquiry into a variety of topics will revitalize and reenergize the group, boosting pride, accomplishment and capacity for ongoing positive transformation.

Aligning Purpose and Goals

Having team goals clearly understood and purpose fully aligned are essential for high performance. Use the following four questions to explore how you have achieved these conditions and how your current team might create even closer alignment and clarity of purpose.

Question 1: When Goals Snap Sharply into Focus

Human organizations rarely achieve peak performance in the absence of clear, compelling goals. When moving towards a fuzzy, approximate destination, it is hard to do our best. Periodically, we become lost in this land of uncertainty; and then suddenly, almost magically, goals snap sharply into focus. Something shifts, and we have a clear vision of where we're headed, along with what individuals and the team needs to do to achieve the goals. Energy is quickly mobilized, aligning team members' efforts for progress.

1. Think back to a time when your team experienced dramatic shift from wandering about to sharply focused goals and purpose. Tell the story of this "magical" moment.

   - Who was involved? How?

   - What really happened? Reflecting back to the time before the shift, and then to the moment(s) when everything changed, what specific elements facilitated the shift?

   - What person or moment stands out, in retrospect, as having stood at the center of the shift? How?

2. It's a week from now. A current team goal that has previously been surrounded by confusion has snapped sharply into focus, bringing with it an infusion of energy and enthusiasm.

   - What's been resolved?

   - How?

   - In particular, what role did you play in making this happen?

Question 2: Challenging Goals, Extraordinary Results

In the life of any team, there are peaks and valleys, times when people miss or barely hit the mark and times when they achieve truly extraordinary results. Extraordinary results don't happen by accident, however. They result, in part, from people's willingness to set, meet and exceed challenging goals.

1. Tell me about a time when this team worked to achieve an extremely challenging goal and in the process achieved extraordinary results. It may have been an episode during your tenure, or it may be part of the group's "oral history."

    - What was the situation?

    - Who established the goals? How?

    - What role did the original goals play in promoting the outcome you've just described?

    - How did people on the team feel about their accomplishments?

2. You've fallen into a magical sleep, and awakened to a celebration five years from today. Your team has just achieved a truly extraordinary result, something that you have always wished you could be part of, that makes an enormous difference in the quality of goods or services that you provide.

    - What has your team achieved? How?

    - How has this extraordinary outcome enhanced the quality of your life, your organization's life, and the life of the people you serve?

    - What was the original goal that was set, five years ago, that set the wheels in motion for the outcome that's now being celebrated?

    - Who was involved in setting that challenging goal? How?

Question 3: For the Good of the Whole

First and foremost, a team is a group of people who come together and function cooperatively to achieve a common purpose. Thus, effective teamwork consists in part of communal selflessness, a collective setting aside of personal agendas and desires, for the good of the whole.

Focusing on and working for the good of the whole gives us a sense of expansion, of moving beyond ourselves, of being part of something large. We come to know and appreciate the joy of the "we," and the increased capacity that comes from joining our efforts with like-minded others.

1. Tell me about a time when you've chosen to set aside personal gain for the good of the whole and have been grateful for having done so.

    -   What internal dynamics within the team or organization encouraged selflessness in both you and others? In other words, how were actions taken for the good of the whole both nurtured and encouraged?

    -   What more did you gain as a result of your decision?

2. What aspects of your current team's or organization's mission or purpose most inspires you to partner with your teammates and work for the good of the whole?

3. What would inspire you to act even more frequently in service of the whole?

Question 4: In the Service of Society

When teams work in the service of society, people feel satisfied and fulfilled. Instead of just making money or overcoming personal challenges, team members are striving to achieve a higher purpose. Day-to-day difficulties shrink to insignificance. Teams are less concerned with their personal agendas and are continually re-energized by focusing on questions of service and legacy. They achieve a sense of unity with their teammates and with the organization as a whole.

1. Describe a time when you were part of a team that worked in the service of society. It may have been part of the team's overall mission, or it may have been a single project or initiative, a kind of "service project."

    - What was the situation? How did it come about? Who was involved?

    - Describe the most positive effects that this focus on a higher purpose had on individual team members—and overall team performance?

2. If this were a short-term project...

    - How were people's attitudes, approaches or relationships different from "business as usual?"

    - What long-term effect did the project have on individuals, and on overall team performance? In other words, what did the team gain from this act of service?

3. What three possible ways can you imagine your team working in the service of society, beginning tomorrow? These could involve small projects or a significant shift in strategic direction.

Clarifying Roles and Responsibilities

Evolving clear roles and responsibilities is another bedrock competency of great teams. These next six questions can help your team think about where you are in this dimension and how you can create even more clarity about the best ways to fit together. One pivotal aspect that supports this ability is conscious knowledge of various working styles.

Question 5: Strengths Working in Synergy

When teams are at their best, they regularly surpass expectations and break new ground, bringing their members a sense of enlargement, transcendence and pride. Such groundbreaking synergy becomes possible when individual team members fully recognize, appreciate and engage one another's complementary strengths and talents. With wholehearted commitment to a shared goal, team members freely contribute what they can when they can, gracefully inviting others to do the same.

1. Describe a time when you and others combined your talents in ways that enhanced everyone's effectiveness.

    - What talents did you and others bring to the table?

    - What enabled you to build on one another's strengths so effectively?

    - What was it about you, your teammates and the overall team environment that facilitated this synergy?

    - What did the team achieve that it could not when these strengths were operating independently?

2. What does this experience teach you about strengths working in synergy? What fosters such high levels of collaboration and performance?

3. Think of one of the more complex challenges your team is facing today.

    - How can you personally apply what you've just described to positively transform how your team is approaching this situation?

- What can you do to encourage other members of your team to more synergistically build on one another's strengths and talents?

Question 6: Enlarging the Team Gracefully

When new people join an existing team, the sense of order and balance shifts. The process of integrating new members can be disruptive or it can happen effortlessly. When it works well, old and new members alike move quickly into a wonderful new rhythm, building on the best of their past while remaining curious about and open to what they can do together. It is a kind of love at first sight experience: an intuitive knowing, accepting and valuing that create a sense of limitless possibilities.

1. Think about the best experience you've had with enlarging a team gracefully. What was it about the individuals and the team as a whole that allowed it to welcome the new member with open arms?

    • What qualities were present in the new teammate that allowed him/her to accept the welcome gracefully?

    • Describe specific moments and particular behaviors that helped smooth out any rough edges.

2. Suppose you could have any three wishes granted that would enable your team to enlarge gracefully. What would they be?

Question 7: Balancing the Skills of Introversion and Extroversion

Introverts gain comfort from private space and time; they draw energy from solitary activities and quiet reflection. In contrast, extroverts are energized through direct contact with people. Some people operate at the extremes of these polar opposite styles much of the time. Others may shift along the introversion-extroversion spectrum depending on their mood, recent events or changing conditions in the environment.

In the life of any team, there are times for introverting and times for extroverting. The greater the complexity of the project, the more a team needs the flexibility of a range of styles.

1. Reflect back to a time in the life of this team when optimal performance required a balance of introverted and extroverted behaviors. It may have called team members to balance these skills within themselves; or it may have required conscious balancing of different people's skills in service of the whole.

    • What was the situation?

    • Who was involved?

    • How did the style(s) of the person(s) involved contribute to the success?

    • What in the team climate helped to support people's individual strengths while balancing out their shortcomings?

2. What current project might benefit from the deliberate balancing of introversion or extroversion? How, specifically, might we go about fostering that balance?

Question 8: Optimizing the Strengths of Intuition and Sensing

Winning teams require world-class decisions that are firmly grounded both in fact and intuition, history and possibility. Team members with the strength of sensing are practical and firmly grounded in facts and experience; they are skilled, accurate observers of the way things are. By contrast, people whose strength is intuition focus on and take in a sense of the whole, often gravitating towards images of possibility.

These distinct approaches to gathering information can clash, creating conflict and confusion within a team. But together, they have the capacity for complex thinking, leading to holographic decision-making. Winning teams learn how to optimize the strengths of intuition and sensing, providing people freedom to dive into the chaos and forge ahead without a clear blueprint, all the while returning to the solid ground of clear-headed, grounded, actionable tactics. Encouragement and leveraging of these strengths unleashes a kind of sensible magic that fuels team progress.

1. Think of a time when your team grappled with a task using both sensing and intuition, alternately or in an oscillating blend. Tell the story of what happened.

   - What were the specifics of the project? What aspects of the work seemed to call for each style?

   - What structures or processes did you use to specifically draw out people's stylistic strengths, or to facilitate a shift in overall team thinking?

   - What was the outcome for the individuals involved and for the team as a whole?

2. What did you learn from this experience that can be applied in future projects, where both steady sensing and wide-open intuition are needed?

Question 9: Leveraging the Capabilities of Thinking and Feeling

The way members arrive at decisions has a huge effect on team progress. People with a *thinking preference* prefer impersonal, intellectual, and rule-governed decisions. In contrast, those who prefer *feeling* make choices based on people, feelings, values, and personal impact. Each decision-making style has is strengths, and each is a precious team asset.

Sometimes the high standards and logical analysis of thinkers lead teams toward well-grounded, deeply considered strategies. At other times, personal and passionate feelers energize the group and ensure that the human dimension is included. Perhaps more often, good decisions take into consideration both the heart and the mind, leveraging people's objective and subjective capacities.

1. Think, now, about your various teammates' styles of approaching decisions and experiences. Recall a time when each played out this strength to overall team advantage.

   • What was the situation?

   • Who did what? To what effect?

2. When have you seen these two styles work together well? Perhaps it was a team when people overtly negotiated the use of a particular style or combination of approaches.

   • What factors (either among the team members or in the overall team climate) enabled the styles to co-exist and coordinate with each other?

3. In thinking of such successful coordination, what kinds of decisions or projects are especially well suited for each of these decision-making styles?

Question 10: Utilizing the Best of Judging and Perceiving

People with a *judging* preference value closure; they like having decisions made so they can move on with a job. Experiencing great satisfaction in the glow of completion, they hungrily and easily set and meet deadlines and objectives. Those with a *perceiving* preference are more comfortable with improvisation and works in progress. Immersing themselves in the quest for information and choices, they hold off on making choices as long as possible.

While such differences can lead to misunderstanding, they can actually maximize team progress. Winning teams know how to utilize the best of judging and perceiving.

1. Describe a time in your work or your life when your personal preference on this dimension has contributed to the best possible outcome for you and others.

2. Now, describe a time when you've stretched beyond your preference and in so doing have contributed to a better outcome than would otherwise have been possible.

3. Describe one of the more positive experiences you've had of successful partnership with someone of the opposite style.

    • How did your differences contribute to everyone's well being?

    • What strategies did you have for utilizing the differences?

    • How did your strategy work?

    • What more might you have done in order to achieve an even more positive outcome?

Fostering Supportive and Empowering Relationships

The moment-by-moment "rules of engagement" for conversations among team members determine the quality of work relationships. These next 10 questions can help you clearly define the positive core of your collaborative relationships and expand those elements to more fully support a positive team climate.

Question 11: An Environment of Trust

All teamwork requires trust among team members—trust that you can depend on one another, that all members will pitch in and do their share of the work, that resources will be fairly distributed, and that everyone will be included and kept informed through open, honest communication. In successful teams, an environment of trust is consciously established and maintained. It becomes a felt presence, an accepted norm and a foundation for all that the team does.

1. Think about all the teams you have been on. Tell me about one that you would say is/was characterized by an environment of trust. Describe the team and what it does/did.

    - How was an environment of trust established?

    - How did you know an environment of trust was present?

2. What were the benefits of the environment of trust…

    - to team members?

    - to the work they were doing?

    - to their organization?

3. What can we learn from this team that might help our current team build a stronger environment of trust?

Question 12: Being a Team Player

At their best, teams are made up of people who like being team players and are good at it. They demonstrate skills such as including others and keeping them informed, making decisions jointly, sharing responsibilities and keeping their promises to team members. They are able to realize personal desires while serving the good of the team. In essence, their personal preference is collaboration and teamwork.

1. Think about someone you consider to be a great team player and tell a story about how she demonstrated her abilities.

    * What made him a great team player?

2. What do you value about yourself as a team player?

    * Tell me about a time when you displayed several of your finest team qualities.

3. If you were the counselor at a camp to teach children to be team players, what and how would you teach them?

Question 13: Courage to Collaborate

It is not always easy to collaborate. At times it takes courage to collaborate. Sometimes it seems as if your needs and wants are opposed to those with whom you are to collaborate. Sometimes it seems that there are not enough resources to go around. And sometimes it seems as if it will take too much time to collaborate and yet you do. It is at these times that you display the courage to collaborate, the willingness to align your needs and wants with others, the commitment to serve the greater good of the whole and the conviction that the only way to create a sustainable world is through collaboration.

1. Tell me about a time when you courageously chose to collaborate and the results were profoundly positive.

    • What was the situation?

    • Why did it take courage for you to collaborate?

    • What were the results?

2. Imagine a world full of collaboration.

    • What would businesses look like?

    • What would they do?

    • How would they be structured?

    • What would leadership be like?

3. How can your courage to collaborate help your team be more effective right now?

Question 14: Transforming Opposition into Collaboration

All teams run into opposition. It is inevitable. The more diversity among team members, the greater the complexity of the team's work and the tighter the resources available to the team, the more likely that opposition will emerge. Interesting, high performance teams thrive on opposition that includes differences in opinions, approaches, ideas and styles of working. The transformation of opposition into collaboration enriches team potential to achieve its goals and get desired results.

1. Tell me about a time when you were on a team that transformed opposition into collaboration.

   - What was the situation?

   - What oppositions emerged and how were they transformed?

   - Who was involved and what skills did they demonstrate that enabled the transformation to occur?

2. Imagine a school where transformation of opposition into collaboration is part of the curriculum.

   - What would be taught?

   - To whom?

Question 15: Reconciliation and Rebuilding Trust

When teams work at their best, members trust one another to be reliable and mutually supportive. But conflict, rifts or misunderstandings can interrupt this ease-filled, trusting atmosphere; and when they do, the important work of reconciliation begins. Reconciliation rebuilds trust and renews bonds. At its best, it leaves teams stronger and more capable than before.

1. Think about a time when you went through a process of reconciliation and rebuilding trust. It may have been on this team or elsewhere in your life. Tell the story.

   • Who was involved?

   • What happened?

   • What specifically did you and the others involved do to work through what needed attention and how did this strengthen your relationship?

   • What did you learn from this process—about yourself, the other person, and trust?

2. Now, describe a time when members of this team have successfully reconciled difficulties or differences, rebuilding trust in the process.

   • Who did what?

   • How?

   • With what effect?

3. Reflecting on these and other experiences that you've had in the past, what are the core factors that contribute to reconciliation and trust? What are the core capacities that you bring to this team in its ongoing commitment to reconciliation and trust?

Question 16: Quietly Inspiring Sacrifices for the Team

Every now and then, individual team members' most outstanding contributions are almost completely invisible. Someone in a peripheral position, or who deliberately shuns the spotlight, steps past the need for acknowledgment and recognition to unobtrusively, almost imperceptibly, give of themselves in service of the team. In the intensity of day-to-day life, such giving can go unrecognized. But such quiet sacrifices can inspire the team and organization, if only the story is revealed.

1. Describe an unselfish, nearly unrecognized sacrifice that made a significant and positive contribution to your team or organization. Who made the sacrifice?

   • What motivated them?

   • What was the outcome for you, and for the team?

2. How might your team take notice of this and similar sacrifices in ways that inspire others and make self-sacrifice a team value?

Question 17: Pulling Together When You Want to Pull Apart

Times of stress or challenge can sometimes pull people and teams apart. But teams that lead the pack find ways of pulling together, even when they want to pull apart. By pulling together against the odds, people in these teams achieve higher levels of performance and satisfaction. Pulling together has intrinsic rewards.

1. Tell me about a time when you really wanted to pull apart from someone but pulled together in a way that led to a truly positive outcome. It may have been a situation on a team or with a family member or friend.

    • What were all the contributing circumstances that enabled you and the other person(s) to pull together, despite your instinctive desire to pull apart?

    • What conversation(s) do you recall having had with yourself, as you were making the decision to move beyond your obstacle?

    • What were the most positive, most productive shifts toward a more collaborative frame of mind? Towards a more collaborative set of actions?

    • What outside support did you receive, if any, that helped you to pull together?

    • What was the outcome?

2. As you reflect on this and other episodes of its kind, what does it take for people to pull together when they really want to pull apart?

3. What is the single greatest gift that you bring to those of us who are working to pull together in the future?

Question 18: Getting to Know You

People who make up great teams get to know each other personally and professionally. The team will thrive as each member learns about one another's interests, what each cares about and what each values. Members learn about each other's families, hobbies and non-work interests and affiliations. They get to know one another's relational, technical and team strengths. By getting to know one another, they create a team bond that will enable them to work together easily by drawing on their respective interests, values and strengths. Team respect, trust and camaraderie all grow as members get to know each other.

1. Tell me about a time in your life when you felt truly energized and alive, either at work or beyond. Describe it in rich detail, so that we can experience it just as you did.

2. Now, think of the person with whom you've most enjoyed working in the past, such as a favorite colleague who might also have been a friend.

   • What did that person know and appreciate about you that helped him or her to be such an important person in your life?

3. Step into the shoes of all the people who most respect and value you, both in the workplace and at home. Through their eyes tell us about yourself.

   • What matters to you the most?

   • What are your favorite pastimes and hobbies?

   • What are your greatest skills and competencies?

   • What makes you tick?

Question 19: Competing Cooperatively

Tenacious competing is at the heart of the American ethos. It can be a tremendous asset for a team, as those who relish competition inspire one another to reach new heights. This kind of competitive climate is especially familiar, and often productive, when the team is competing against outside rivals.

How do we work when our rivals are our partners? How do we create an environment of cooperative competition that stimulates commitment and focus, pushes us beyond what we thought were our limits, and builds good will and high performance across the value chain? In the heat of competition, we urge one another on with considerate one-upsmanship, striving to win while supporting those we surpass in performing to their full capacities.

1. Describe a time that you either experienced or heard of when rivals worked with one another in the spirit of competitive cooperation.

    • What were the circumstances?

    • Specifically, how did team members balance competition and cooperation in their quest for mutual excellence?

2. If there was a specific moment when team members were both hard-nosed competitors and nurturing collaborators, describe it in depth.

    • How did they demonstrate each of these attitudes and actions?

    • What were the results for both the relationship(s) and the project(s) when all was said and done?

3. Now, consider your current team.

    • In what single area would you most benefit from a more balanced mix of cooperative competition? (It may be within the team, or between this team and another organization.)

    • How might you go about promoting that shift to competitive cooperation?

Question 20: Breakthrough Collaboration

Every so often people combine their talents in such a way that their effectiveness skyrockets. Such breakthrough collaboration is often unplanned. Instead, something special, even mysterious, happens, almost (though not completely) by accident. Participants and the team itself enlarge; individuals feel connected to something much larger and more meaningful than themselves.

1. Thinking back over the entire course of your career, recall a time when you were part of this kind of breakthrough collaboration.

    *   Who were all the conscious contributors? What was it about you, your co-workers, the goals, the environment, that paved the way for this extraordinary outcome?

    *   Who were all the accidental contributors?

2. Knowing what you know now from this and similar experiences, what are the core factors that contribute to breakthrough collaboration?

3. When your team is at its best, what does it already do to foster breakthrough collaboration?

4. What more could the team do, in order for this to be the norm?

Creating Clear and Shared Procedures

When patterns of planning and decision-making within a team are clear, work progresses smoothly. The next four questions explore the elements that you need to enhance your team procedures so meetings and projects flow better.

Question 21: Exceptional Follow-Through

Exceptional follow-through means saying what we will do and doing what we say. It means doing whatever it takes to meet our commitments.

When each member of this team demonstrates exceptional follow-through, we can count on one another's support as we rise to meet the challenges of our individual and collective responsibilities. Being clear about what's possible, we stretch ourselves to our fullest capacities. We trust and are trusted, appreciate and are appreciated. When we demonstrate exceptional follow through, we enjoy a sense of pride and accomplishment.

1. Describe a time when you and this team demonstrated exceptional follow-through in spite of obstacles. What was it about this situation that fostered such extraordinary follow-through?

   • How did you enter into your commitment in the first place?

   • How did you communicate along the way?

   • How did you and other individual players manage yourselves along the way?

   • What kind of additional support did you need in order to say what you would do, and do what you said?

2. Reflecting on this and other episodes you've experienced, witnessed, or heard about, what systems, structures and processes contribute to exceptional follow-through?

3. Now, consider a challenge or obstacle that you or we are dealing with today. What's the most positive possible outcome you can imagine if we demonstrate that same level of follow-through in this particular situation?

How can you and we leverage what we know about exceptional follow-through to ensure that outcome?

Question 22: Full Voice Decision-Making

The best decisions are full voice decisions. Full voice decisions involve all who are affected and all whose insights can help. They unfold as individual decision makers engage in relationships and conversations that invite their full voice including experience and ideas, mind and heart, curiosities, questions and concerns.

1. Describe a time when you were engaged in a full voice decision that resulted in the best possible outcome for you, the other parties, and the task itself. It may have been here on this team or elsewhere in your life.

    • What was the situation, and how did it unfold?

    • Who was involved? How?

    • What was the outcome?

2. Specifically, what made this full voice decision different and better than other decisions of its kind that you've seen or experienced?

3. Suppose you had the power to make full voice decision-making the norm within this particular team.

    • What would you need to do more of?

    • What would you need to change?

    • What first steps would you take in order to move us solidly in the direction of what you've just described? How?

Question 23: Meetings That Make a Difference

Meetings can enrich our lives and work, or they can drain away time from the things that matter most. When they are at their best, meetings make a positive difference in how we team. They help us to do what we do, better, more efficiently and in ways that are more fulfilling.

1. Describe the best meeting you've ever experienced a meeting that really made a difference for you, your team and the work you were trying to achieve.

    *   What was it about you, the situation and the meeting itself that made this a pivotal gathering?

    *   What was the outcome?

    *   Specifically, what role did this and future meetings play in furthering such a positive outcome?

2. Now, describe a meeting that you've participated in within our current team that could have made a difference, but didn't. What could we have done differently that would have enabled that meeting to be the kind of gathering you've just described?

3. What will you do, beginning tomorrow, to help ensure that future meetings make a difference both within our team and across our organization?

Question 24: Exemplary Project Planning

Extraordinary accomplishments don't just happen. They result from exemplary performance within and across teams and functions, often enabled by exemplary project planning. Exemplary project planning brings people and resources together in the right way, at the right time, to achieve extraordinary results.

1. Describe the most exemplary project planning process you've ever seen, experienced, or heard about, one that significantly enhanced a team's or organization's performance and capacities.

    *   What was the situation or task?

    *   Who was involved in the planning? How?

    *   How were resources delegated?

    *   How were tasks identified and assigned?

    *   If the planning process resulted in some sort of physical document or plan, describe the document/plan in as much detail as you can.

    *   Knowing what you know now, in hindsight, how could this planning process have been strengthened even further?

2. Using this and other planning processes as a template, describe in detail your *ideal* project planning process.

3. Suppose that this ideal project planning process were to be applied in this team or organization to one of our stickier and more challenging projects, what would we continue doing, or do more of?

    *   What would be different about the way we would be conducting ourselves? With what effect?

    *   What *first steps* would we be taking today if our intention were to fully adopt this exemplary project planning?

Promoting Leadership

Effective leadership is surely the bedrock of high performing teams. Yet there is a wide spectrum of leadership styles and each team must discover what works best for its unique combination of people. These questions are intended to facilitate exploration of the kinds of leadership best suited for your team

Question 25: Inspiring Leadership

Leadership can make or break a team. When people come together for a common purpose, they need leadership. It can be singular or shared, it can be visionary or action oriented, it can be participatory or charismatic. Team leadership can take many forms as long as it is inspiring leadership that brings out the best in people. Inspiring leadership is a call to action in the service of a higher good. It motivates people to align their needs, wants and strengths toward the common purpose. It gives people hope that what they are doing can succeed and is indeed worthwhile.

1. Tell me about a time when you experienced inspiring leadership. It may have been on a team at work or as a community volunteer. Describe the situation.

    •   Was there one person or a team of inspiring leaders?

    •   What did they do that you found inspiring?

    •   What or who brought out your best?

    •   How did this happen?

2. How has this experience influenced you as a leader? What conscious choices do you make as a result of this inspiring leadership?

3. What might you do to demonstrate more inspiring leadership with your current team?

Question 26: Shared Leadership

Leadership is guidance, the sharing of one's hopes, dreams, aspirations and skills in order to elevate another. Each of us shares leadership, day in and day out, as we bring our dreams to life by investing in a collective future, coaching one another, and contributing our gifts for the higher good. When we formally and informally share leadership, everyone comes alive, engages and contributes to his or her fullest capacities. High performance teams and organizations count on shared leadership to enhance creativity, increase organizational capacity and stimulate performance.

1. Describe two or three examples of successful shared leadership that you've seen or experienced within this particular organization or team. They may have been times when leadership was formally shared, or when there was an informal exchange of thoughts, ideas and skills in service of a common goal.

    - What were the circumstances?

    - Who shared leadership with whom? How?

    - How was leadership passed from one member of the organization or team to another? What made it an effective "hand-off?"

    - How was the final "product" enhanced, as a result of leadership having been shared? In other words, how did shared leadership make our organization or team *better* than it would have otherwise been?

2. Without being humble, what are your greatest strengths as a "leader" in this organization?

3. How do those strengths elevate the people around you? How might you bring those strengths to bear even more fully, as we move towards the future?

Question 27: Leadership That Brings Out Your Best

Leadership makes a difference in people's lives and careers. It paves the way for exemplary performance, or suppresses people's natural gifts and capacities. When leadership brings out our best, it nurtures our strengths, enhances our capacities and alters the course of our destinies in profound and positive ways. It is a cornerstone of exemplary individual and team performance.

1. Describe a peak experience or high point in your career: a time when you felt really alive, engaged, and proud of yourself and your performance.

   • What role did leadership play in this experience?

   • Specifically, how did a leader or leadership practice unleash your capacities, and help you to fulfill your highest calling?

2. Now, describe a time when this team was absolutely at its best.

   • What role did leadership play in this episode?

   • Specifically, how did a leader or leadership practice unleash the team's capacities, and help the group to fulfill its collective calling?

3. Reflecting on these and other experiences, what are the core leadership qualities and practices that bring out the best in you and this team?

4. You now have three wishes that, when granted, will make an extraordinary positive change in leadership's capacity to bring out the best in you and in this team. What are they?

Question 28: Leadership That Engages the Heart

Every person is unique, and so is every leader. Some leaders inspire through intellect, forging new visions and pathways with clear, well-conceived plans and penetrating brainpower. Others engage people's hearts, leading through the power of relationships. They have well-honed abilities to tune in to other people's feelings and needs…to connect with and validate people's experience and knowledge. Leadership that engages the heart forges powerful bonds of empathy, trust and commitment. As people feel validated and supported for who they are, they freely and passionately stretch and grow beyond themselves.

1. Describe a person whom you believe is particularly skillful at "leading from the heart." It may be someone you've worked for or with, or simply someone of whom you've heard.

    • Who is this person?

    • What are the core leadership behaviors that he/she exhibits?

    • Describe a time when that leadership style was particularly helpful—to your development, or the achievement of a group's chosen goal or task. In other words, how did this person's leadership style enhance how people worked and what they accomplished?

2. When your team's current leadership is at its best, what are all the ways in which it engages your heart?

3. *How else* might your team's leadership engage your heart, and the hearts of your co-workers?

Elevating Energy and Spirit

An important part of the appeal of working in teams is the contagious energy and spirit teams generate. Being part of this flow of energy, so much larger than an individual, is profoundly rewarding. The next set of questions delves into the elements that create and sustain this team spirit.

Question 29: Celebrations That Reverberate

Without a doubt teams that celebrate their successes have more successes. And the best celebrations are ones that reverberate. Recognition and celebration can give team members that extra boost of energy or confidence to keep on going when the going gets tough. When team members feel good and the good feeling goes home with them, or to a meeting with a customer, or into an important negotiation they get better results.

1. Think about the teams you have been on and tell me about one that created celebrations that reverberated.

    - How did the team celebrate?

    - What made their celebrations reverberate?

2. Tell me about a time when you were recognized and celebrated.

    - How did you feel?

    - How did it affect the rest of your day? Your relationships with the people who honored you?

3. Imagine a team that celebrates regularly, what would it celebrate? How?

Question 30: The Secret Language of History That Bonds

One of the great pleasures of being part of a group—a class, a family, a summer camp, a team—is creating and enjoying shared history. Going through events together and telling stories about common (yet unique) experiences creates powerful bonds of understanding. Often these shared experiences are captured in images or metaphors that become an ongoing part of the group's identity: a kind of secret language that only teammates share and understand. These images can be used to bring people closer and help them communicate in a sort of private shorthand. They act as a powerful bond, and last long after the group experience is done.

1. What is the "secret language" of your particular team? What are the most positive stories that you tell about yourselves that capture the essence of who you are and how you operate, when you are at your best?

2. When your team is at its best, how do you and others introduce "newcomers" to this secret language? How do you share your history, inviting them to become co-creators of the future?

3. What stories and images would you like your team to be sharing with newcomers, three years from today? What will be the prevailing "secret language" that will reflect the best possible future you can imagine?

Question 31: Jokes That Bind

Humor gives life to human systems. It enables people to experience joy and laughter, and to find hope in the midst of despair. Jokes, in particular, bind people to one another, reinforcing—or in some cases reforming—people's experience of reality. Playful nicknames, for example, deepen people's appreciation for individuals' special qualities. Funny stories of shared experiences remind people of times when they laughed and loved and got things done. Jokes that bind can become a conscious group norm that makes the team more productive...and more fun.

1. Tell me about some of the jokes that bind your team together. Where did these jokes come from? How are they used to enhance people's experience of one another, and enhance the team's performance?

2. What are the core characteristics of a "binding" joke or story?

3. What more could your team do foster loving, uplifting, inspirational humor within its ranks? How might your team build on its communal jokes, to make them even more powerful and/or more fun?

Question 32: Celebrating Our Stars

Many of us get a thrill from winning: from surging ahead into the spotlight ahead of others—perhaps even our colleagues. Powerful individual strengths mean that individual team members will periodically take the lead over others. This can stimulate overall team success, when teams find ways of celebrating the success of their *stars*. Everyone truly and sincerely recognizes and enjoys one another's successes. Everyone commits to helping one another be the best that they can be.

1. What kind of recognition and celebration makes you feel most appreciated by your colleagues and co-workers? What kind of celebration makes you want to be the best you can be, and to freely share your gifts with those around you?

2. Describe two or three "stars" on your team. What are these people's unique skills and gifts? How do their gifts enhance you and the rest of this team—both in the day-to-day work you do, and in the eyes of your customers?

3. It's three years from day, and your team has just been featured in a local news magazine for its remarkable capacity to groom and develop talent. The author of the story describes the exceptional number of "stars" that have come through this team through the years, performing groundbreaking work while remaining deeply connected to and supported by the overall team. Tell the story, through the eyes of this reporter, of how this team celebrates and cultivates individual "stardom" among its members.

Question 33: Praise Unleashes the Power of Pride

Pride is pleasure in our own competence...delight in seeing our efforts make a positive difference. Pride reminds us of our competencies and strengths, encouraging us to use our talents both systematically and strategically.

Praise is a catalyst for pride. It unleashes our power by reminding us that we are seen, valued and needed. It strengthens our sense of trust and solidifies the bonds between us. Praise amplifies individual and collective performance. It gives people confidence, and draws them towards a positive future.

1. Describe a time when you either gave or received praise from one of your teammates.

   • What was said?

   • How was it delivered?

   • What was the immediate effect on the person who was praised? On the giver of the praise?

   • How did the praise seem to impact the work progress?

   • How did it alter the relationship?

2. As you reflect on yourself, your teammates, and your team as a whole, what are you most proud of? What is most valuable or important about the work that you and your teammates do?

3. How is your life—and the life of others—enhanced by this important work?

Question 34: Spirit of Curiosity

Curiosity killed the cat—or did it? Cats explore and take risks, climbing trees where they can see further than others! They are physically flexible. And if you take the risk of dropping them upside down, they will always twist and land on their feet.

1. Please tell me a story about a time in your team when your curiosity—and the curiosity of your teammates—really flowed, stretching everyone to be open to new ideas.

2. What do you personally need to regularly take risks and be experimental?

3. What do you believe your team needs in order to ignite and sustain this spirit of curiosity on an everyday, ordinary basis?

Advancing Productivity and Performance

The following questions examine some of the elements that underlie overall team productivity. This includes exploring what works with the challenges that potentially derail progress.

Question 35: Disciplined Execution

Execution—the missing link between aspirations and results—engages everyone in the discipline of getting things done right, on time, every time. In teams that are strong at disciplined execution, the right people are in the right jobs, and are rewarded for their contributions. Members go beyond their job descriptions, caring more about team success than the defined boundaries of their job. They are continual learners, absorbing whatever knowledge they need for continuous performance improvement.

1. Think about a time when you were proud to be involved with others in the disciplined execution of a work process. Describe the event in detail.

   - What made you proud?

   - Who else was involved?

   - Specifically, what happened during this collaboration that resulted in such disciplined execution?

2. Suppose that tomorrow, your entire team brought that same level of disciplined execution to a generally routine task. Which repetitive task might you choose to focus on?

   - How would that ordinary job be made extraordinary through applying more disciplined execution?

   - How would team members' relationship to one another be different than it has been?

   - How would people's jobs and job performance change?

Question 36: Playful Productivity

Artists know that play and productivity go hand in hand. The creative act is a unique balance of playful exploration and results oriented productivity. Successful teams, too, are able to balance playfulness and productivity. Openness to fun, curiosity and learning contribute a great deal to team vitality and productivity. At the same time a focus on results contributes to a sense of possibility and pride. Playful productivity produces high morale among team members and leads to the innovative accomplishment of goals.

1. Describe a moment of playful productivity, a time when you or your team had a blast getting things done. Tell me about the situation, what you accomplished and how you had fun doing it.

2. If you were asked to recite the code of conduct for playful productivity what would you say?

3. Who do you know that brings playful productivity to teams?

    • What do they do?

    • What can we learn from them to liven up the spirit and boost the results of our team?

Question 37: Turning Pressure into Performance

High performance teams have a way of working hard and playing hard. They are able to keep going when the pressure is on. Indeed they are able to turn pressure—deadlines, complexity, limited resources, and customer demands—into performance. They get results in the face of pressure. And everyone benefits. Customers are happy, the organization achieves its goals and team members are recognized and rewarded—often with another equally challenging project!

1. Think about what causes you pressure and tell me about a time when you successfully turned that pressure into high performance.

    • What was the situation?

    • What did you do?

2. How did you feel as you did this? What were the benefits to you and to others?

3. Imagine your team regularly turning pressure into performance.

    • What pressures are there?

    • How are they each being transformed into successful results?

Question 38: Rapid Recovery from a Setback

Unpredictable and uncontrollable adversity can demoralize and discourage—or it can stimulate and challenge. But even after particularly tough disappointments or setbacks, high performance teams quickly regain their energy and focus. People regroup, seeking hopeful possibilities and new directions for productive action. Sometimes sooner, sometimes later, team members experience the setback as having stimulated necessary learning and sent them into the future even more capable than before.

1. Think back to a time when your team recovered rapidly from a disappointing setback.

    • Who was involved?

    • What happened?

    • What internal or external factors enabled such a rapid recovery?

    • What permanent, positive changes did the team experience as a result of its experience?

2. How can you apply what you learned from that situation? In particular, what first steps can you and your team take towards recovery from a fairly recent disappointment or setback?

Question 39: Teams Triumphing with Technology

Instantly connecting people and ideas across great distance, technology allows teams to access a breadth and depth of resources in ways unimagined even a decade ago. Technology adds great value to teams' capacities, making them more agile, responsive to customers and resilient in the face of adversity. High performance teams know how to leverage these capacities in service of their purpose. High performance teams know how to triumph with technology.

1. What do you most value about your team's current use of technology? What are all the ways in which your performance and quality of life are enhanced because of your triumphant use of this powerful resource?

2. If you could have any three wishes granted to heighten the health and vitality of your team's relationship with technology, what would they be?

Question 40: Doing More with Less

We have all experienced easy times and hard times in our careers: times when money was plentiful and times when budgets had to be cut. Sometimes, when resources are scarce, we are surprised by our capacity to do more with less. We discover best practices that free us up to focus more fully on what really matters, and to consistently efficiently deliver exceptional results.

1. Give me an example of a creative initiative that you've seen, heard of or experienced, that enabled an organization to do more with less.

    • What was the situation?

    • How were the changes conceived and implemented?

    • What was the outcome?

2. Now, describe to me a time that you were proud of, when you joined with others to implement some sort of system or process or change that enabled you or your organization do more with less. What changes did you make? How? What was the impact?

    • What was it about your attitude, your relationships, inter-departmental support, the systems and the structure that enabled you and your colleagues to do more with less?

    • What kinds of communication and coordination were required to support this effort?

3. What are all the opportunities you see—in this team, and in this organization—to do more with less? In what ways might these saved resources (time, money, etc.) enhance...

    • ...this team's and organization's financial performance?

    • ...the quality of the service you provide?

    • ...the overall quality of your life—both at work, and beyond?

Question 41: The Surprise of Success

Though we always hope for and work hard to achieve success, we are occasionally *surprised* by a measure of success that far exceeds our hopes and dreams. Such surprising successes are born of a synchronistic coming-together of people, talents, resources and timing. High-performance teams frequently experience the surprise of success, as they work together in extraordinary ways to achieve extraordinary goals.

1. Describe a time when you were surprised by success—in your work, your family or in a volunteer organization.

    *   What were the circumstances?

    *   What was it about both the team members, and the way that they worked with one another, that brought about that surprising success?

    *   What was the outcome?

    *   How did it feel for those who were involved?

2. Imagine that it is a year from now, and one of the more important projects on which we're currently working—perhaps one about which we've been concerned—has turned out to be a tremendous and surprising success.

    *   How is the outcome of that project better or more compelling than what we'd originally hoped for?

    *   What were all the positive contributing circumstances that came together to create that surprise of success?

    *   What did members of this team do to bring about or influence those positive contributing circumstances?

    *   Specifically, how did *you* use your skills, talents and influence to contribute to that surprise of success?

    *   Looking back from the future, what is the most positive difference that this outcome has made for you, your work and your life?

Question 42: Mining Your Assortment of Winning Styles and Temperaments

Each of us has preferred pathways for tackling tasks. Working with and within our personal style brings us ease and comfort, and the capacity to fully engage our strengths.

Teams often agree on goals, but frequently differ on how to go about getting the job done. Every team member's unique style captures special strengths that contribute to collective performance. A piccolo and the double bass sound and look radically different, yet each unique tone adds to the rich sound of the whole orchestra. Similarly, in daily team life diverse styles move on and off center stage, dancing separately and together in constantly shifting rhythms and combinations. How smoothly this choreographed chaos flows is one measure of team effectiveness. The following questions are intended to help you clarify how styles contribute to your team experience. With increased awareness and appreciation of the power of these differences, teams can create climates that allow all styles to thrive, complement and contribute.

1. Describe a time when stylistic differences within your team were particularly pronounced—and particularly useful.

    *   What was the situation?

    *   Who was involved?

    *   How did different team members' unique styles contribute to a positive outcome?

    *   How did you and other members of the team *consciously mine* the value of these differences?

2. Looking back at this and similar situations that you've experienced in the past, what are the core factors that contribute to a team's capacity to mine the most positive aspects of its members' styles and temperaments?

Question 43: Driving Force

When we tap into our passions (what turns us on) we become fueled and receive power to move beyond our present reality with determination and commitment to do whatever it takes. Winning teams, too, are impelled to perform by the driving force of passion.

1. Describe a time in your work with your team when your passion was ignited, and you moved out of neutral, got into gear and moved toward a goal.

    *   What was the situation?

    *   Who was involved?

    *   What was the driving force behind that movement? Specifically, what role did your teammates, and/or the work of the team itself, play in helping you to *move?*

2. As you look towards this team's future, what images or possibilities most excite you? How does this excitement propel you to act in service of the whole?

Stimulating Purposeful and Uplifting Communication

Communication is, quite literally, the lifeblood of a team. Only through effective exchange of meaning can team members coordinate their strengths and achieve their goals. Since communication is so basic, we may take it for granted. The questions in this set are aimed at examining more closely how communication works at its best.

Question 44: Teeming with Emotional Intelligence

The complex challenges of our world demand technical and intellectual competence—but also some thing much more important. "Emotional intelligence"—the capacity for self-awareness, empathy, self-control, clear listening, and assertive self-expression—is now recognized as a pivotal predictor of professional success. .

High performance teams are teeming with emotional intelligence. Over and over again, individual team members put the best of their knowledge into play, joining with one another to foster trusting, collaborative relationships that outlive even the most challenging of circumstances.

1. Think back to a time of high demand and high pressure within your team, when one or more people's exceptional emotional intelligence allowed a clear decision to emerge, helped the team see a great new strategy, or allowed teammates to put their minds together and get the job done.

    • What were the circumstances?

    • What kind of emotionally intelligent behavior did you see? Specifically how did you or another person rise above the chaos?

    • What difference did this make to the overall team's effectiveness?

    • As you reflect on this and other episodes of its kind, what personal or group factors contributed to this occurrence of emotional intelligence?

2. It's a year from today, and your team is simply *teeming* with emotional intelligence. What's the same as it was, a year before?

    - What's different?

    - What first steps did you team take, a year ago, to plant the seeds for even more emotionally intelligent behaviors among its members?

Question 45: Open and Honest Communication

A team is an intimate place. To work closely with others, especially those committed to the highest performance, means revealing essential details about who we are, what we know and what we believe. We put our ideas, values and passions on the line with our teammates—and we hold our teammates gently as they do the same. In order to foster such intimacy and high performance, we need regular, open, honest, communication. When information flows freely, we can pool our strengths and make progress toward our mutual goals.

1. Describe a time when you were particularly proud of an open, honest exchange that took place between you and another person—at work, or elsewhere in your life.

  • What made the exchange possible?

  • Specifically, what was it about you, the other person, or the situation that opened the door for what took place?

2. If there was some kind of pronounced shift in this exchange—from defensive or partial communication to openness and honesty—what made that shift possible? What was it about you, the other person or the people around you that enabled such a transformation?

3. What three small changes could you and your teammates agree to, that together would enhance the level of open and honest communication within the team?

Question 46: Listening to Understand

Being listened to and authentically understood is one of the most powerful human experiences. When people really listen to us, setting aside their personal stories in order to deeply understand our experience, they join us in our world. For at least that moment, any sense of separateness dissolves, and our willingness to contribute increases. As we join with our teammates in this bubble of understanding, each of us willingly offers up our unique thoughts, ideas insights and gifts. Listening to understand strengthens team performance.

1. Describe a time when you really listened to understand another person.

    • What specific behaviors did you exhibit?

    • What kind of inner dialogue did you engage in? In other words, what went on *inside your head* that helped you to listen with this kind of rapt attention and intention?

    • What was the outcome? In other words, how did the other person respond to you?

2. Now, describe a time when someone else listened to you, with that same intentionality.

    • What was the effect on you?

    • How did that episode alter or enhance the relationship between you and this other person?

    • What specifically did each of you do to facilitate deep understanding?

3. If you could have three wishes granted to enliven people's capacities for listening and genuine understanding within this team, what would they be?

Question 47: Snatching Consensus from the Jaws of Dissension

In the face of important decisions, the stakes seem higher than usual. Everyone wants to have input; everyone wants to make a difference. With a sense of urgency, people can begin defending their own unique perspectives, even to the point of stepping on others' toes. Yet sometimes a shift occurs, away from contentiousness towards cooperation and consensus. People take the time to listen…to engage in ways that invite constructive dissent, along with the discovery of shared goals and perspectives. Like a phoenix rising from the ashes, consensus is snatched from the jaws of dissension. Everyone feels proud of and invested in the outcome, and keenly connected to the team.

1. Tell me about a time—on this team or elsewhere—when you were part of a group that snatched consensus from the jaws of dissension.

   • What was the situation?

   • How did you, the group's norms or practices, or specific members turn things around and steer the group toward a consensus? How was this momentum maintained?

2. Now, consider a somewhat contentious decision that your team is currently working through.

   • What needs to happen, in order for your team to arrive at a solid, well thought-out consensus?

   • Specifically, what can *you* do to make that happen?

Question 48: Seamless Cross-team Collaboration

Cross-team collaboration is a fact of life in today's organizational settings. The complexity of tasks and the interdependence of functions make it important, if not crucial, that people work well with one another through an entire organization. High performance teams make this necessary collaboration seem seamless. Everyone communicates both smoothly and completely. Everyone seeks out and leverages other people's knowledge and talents. It's as if the teams are temporarily enlarged—their boundaries suddenly expanded, their capacities increased.

1. Describe a time when you experienced this kind of seamless cross-team collaboration, either on your existing team—or elsewhere, in another organization.

    *   Who was involved?

    *   How?

    *   What made this collaboration important or necessary?

2. What systems, practices and individual strengths made this experience so successful?

    *   Specifically, what did members of your team do to make the relationships and communication flow easily and fully?

    *   How did people from both teams integrate the needed resources?

Section 4:
Positive Team Development: A Self-Managed Appreciative Inquiry

Coming together is a beginning.
Keeping together is progress.
Working together is success.

—Henry Ford

There comes a time in the life of every team when time out for reflection makes sense. When the team needs to stop action, members should learn from what they have been doing and make decisions about how they want to go forward as a team. This is an opportunity for team development—the collaborative consideration of how the team operates, why it exists and how it can better deliver on the promise of its purpose.

The need for team development may come about when a team faces a new and exciting opportunity and wants to get all its ducks in a row before going forward. It may arise following a great success or team accomplishment when team members start asking, "Now what do we do? Where do we go from here?" It may stem from the inclusion of new members on the team and the need to clarify roles and responsibilities. Or it may simply come from a growing sense that "we could be working together better."

No matter what creates the need, team development is a natural process. The most effective teams in business, service, sports and the arts take time to learn from what they do and to focus upon doing it better. Teams are a collection of relationships; and like all relationships, they thrive when they are nurtured through conscious inquiry and dialogue.

In this chapter we provide an outline for *positive team development*. The process is designed to help you use the positive questions in this book and to conduct an appreciative inquiry into your team's best practices, positive core and visions for the future. By using the questions in this book, you will foster dialogue among team members that brings out their best and invites them to focus on a positive future together.

When to Use This Process

The process outlined on the following pages can be useful when the following occur:

- Your team has just completed a major initiative and wants to debrief and learn from its success.

- You have recently added new people to the team.

- You have been given a new, challenging assignment and must organize to accomplish it.

- Your team is experiencing conflict.

- Your team needs to get its act together in order to work collaboratively with other teams, departments or functions.

- Your team needs to focus on its customers and redesign what it does and how it operates.

- Your team has been working long and hard and needs some time to celebrate.

The process is designed to be self-managed, though under some circumstances you might choose to have it led by a facilitator. If your team is working well together (i.e., members can speak their hearts and minds openly to one another and are comfortable with respectful disagreement), your team can very likely proceed with a self-managed process. Assuming that everyone on the team agrees to self-manage, you will all experience a sense of positive renewal from the inquiry and from sharing and reflecting on best practices.

To give your team the most positive experience possible, we suggest that each time you meet you select people for each of the following three roles:

1. Discussion Leader—manages the agenda, keeps the discussion on topic, and ensures that everyone gets to talk.

2. Timekeeper—keeps track of time and helps the group to ensure that conversations occur within agreed upon time frames.

3. Recorder—documents discussions as they occur, recording key decisions, commitments and action plans.

When to Use a Facilitator

Facilitators are people who are not team members, who have agreed to guide the team through a meeting or a series of meetings. Skilled facilitators make sure that the team's time together is relevant and interesting to everyone involved, and that everyone has equal airtime.

If your team is currently in a state of conflict or significant transition, we recommend you consider asking a facilitator to lead you through the process. A skilled facilitator can guide the team through "rough waters," clearing the way for team harmony and high performance.

The Process of Positive Team Development

The ten steps in this self-managed team Appreciative Inquiry process include the following:

1. Selecting questions and adapting them to your team situation.

2. Deciding who will be interviewed and by whom.

3. Conducting appreciative interviews.

4. Sharing data and stories as a whole team.

5. Mapping your team's positive core.

6. Envisioning your team's future.

7. Articulating your team's purpose.

8. Creating a set of guiding principles.

9. Clarifying roles, relationships and responsibilities for going forward together.

10. Celebrating together.

The steps in this process are designed to help your team move forward in its development. Team development begins with members getting to know one another. As they get to know each other professionally and personally, they bond and form a sense of shared identity. Team members' language shifts from *I* to *we*, and the team becomes something more than the sum of its parts. Steps 1–5 will support your team in this developmental process.

Having created a sense of *we*, team members often begin to test one another's commitment to the team and to each other. They question why things are being done the way they are done. In such circumstances, the team will be served by a clear purpose, and/or or a set of guiding principles for how things will get done. Similarly, people might seek to clarify roles, responsibilities and relationships within the team and with stakeholders. Steps 6–9 will help your team with these key developmental needs.

And of course, all successful teams need to be sure their inner dialogue stays at a 5 to 1 ratio of positive to negative team talk. Step 10 will help you celebrate and create ways for ongoing celebration and sustainability of an appreciative team consciousness.

While each step in this process is important, you may find that some are more relevant than others at a particular time in the life of your team. Feel free to adapt the steps to meet your unique team needs. Whatever you do, be sure to begin with appreciative interviews, using questions from this book or similar ones that you create as a team. Always, always, always start with appreciative interviews.

Step 1: Selecting Questions and Adapting Them to Your Team

Teams, like every human system, move in the direction of what they study, what they ask questions about, analyze and discuss. Therefore, the selection of questions to guide your inquiry and team development process is a very important first step.

Selecting questions may require that you shift your focus from what's wrong with your team to what you want to learn about and develop within your team. For example, instead of trying to resolve a team conflict, select questions that explore resources leading to greater cooperation. Rather than diagnosing the causes of turnover, explore how to expand the conditions that support meaningful team engagement. Instead of trying to solve the problem of low morale, choose questions that help you discover the root causes of high performance. This shift from problems to possibilities sustains energy and excitement, and builds team wisdom and capability. Choose your questions carefully, focusing on those qualities that you want more of within your team.

We suggest that each member of your team review the forty-eight questions in this book, selecting two questions that best express what she hopes the team can become. Have everyone share his two chosen questions and explain why he believes the qualities are important to the development of the team. After hearing from each and every team member, make note of any overlaps and narrow the list of possibilities.

Recognizing that an effective inquiry requires three to five questions, reduce the list generated by the team. Give team members time to talk about the questions and what they mean, sharing with one another why they believe one might be more appropriate or useful than another. Then see how many you have.

In the end, you may narrow down the list by voting. Give team members three votes each, and ask them to cast them for the three topics they sense are most important to the team's future. Repeat this process as many times as necessary in order to narrow the list down to the top three to five topics.

Once you select the three to five questions that will guide your positive team development process, be sure to review them and re-write them in any way necessary to fit the unique requirements of your team's purpose and environment. Then turn to Section 5 and create an interview guide using your questions.

Now, review your interview guide carefully. Be sure that it has a balance of questions (e.g., positive past experiences, reflection and meaning making, and hopes and dreams for the team's future). The information and stories you collect will be used to map your team's positive core, based on past high point experiences, and to create a team purpose and set of guiding principles based on hopes and dreams for the future.

Step 2: Deciding Who Will Be Interviewed and by Whom

Having selected the questions, you will need to decide whom you will interview. At a minimum, you will want to interview all team members. In addition, we suggest you have team members interview people from outside of the team. Outside stakeholders who interact with your team on a regular basis will have valuable perspectives on your team, its strengths and its developmental opportunities.

To identify which stakeholders you might want to interview, draw a map of your value chain—all the people who provide value to or gain value from the work of your team. Consider for example, a product development team. Its value chain might include engineering, materials management, suppliers of raw materials, customers, marketing and sales, as well as senior management. As a team, discuss your value chain and identify representatives from each stakeholder group to be interviewed.

After deciding whom you will interview, decide who will conduct which interviews. Appreciative interviews are a great way to build relationships and shared knowledge across functional lines or lines of authority. They can also serve as a cross training experience and help team members understand the challenges each other faces on a daily basis. For these reasons we recommend that you have team members interview stakeholders with whom they do not generally work.

Everyone on the team should conduct at least one interview with another team member. If stakeholder interviews are conducted, be sure that all team members conduct at least one stakeholder interview as well. An equal distribution of the interviews is important for all team members to have an equal voice later in the process when interview data and key lessons are shared.

Step 3: Conducting Appreciative Interviews

Now that you have a list of people to interview and a plan for who will interview whom, team members will conduct the interviews. Appreciative interviews provide a wonderful forum for discovery, learning and relationship building. People like recalling stories of past successes and sharing hopes and dreams for the future. When asked affirmative questions, such as the ones in this book, people feel safe to share what most matters to them. As a result, appreciative interviews are energizing, both for the people who are interviewed and the interviewers themselves.

Appreciative interviews vary in length, depending on the number of questions you ask. The average interview takes somewhere between 45 and 60 minutes, plus an additional five to ten minutes for post-interview summaries. Be sure to allow enough time so that neither interviewers nor interviewees feel rushed or pressured by time. Effective appreciative interviews are as much about the experience of storytelling and relationship making as they are about the information and data collected. This requires a relaxed atmosphere guided by a spirit of inquiry.[10]

The Spirit of Inquiry

The most important quality of an appreciative interview is the spirit of inquiry—the willingness to listen and learn from your interviewee. Chet Bowling, a colleague at Ohio State University, suggests that the best appreciative interviews are conducted with the openness, playfulness and in-the-moment aliveness of a five-year old. When conducting your appreciative interviews, let a curious five-year-old's sense of wonder be your guide.

Focus on Stories

Another important point to keep in mind is the centrality of stories. Your focus as an interviewer is to create a safe space for stories to emerge. Through attentive listening and empathy, you will be able to draw out the best of your interviewee. Remember you are there to draw out and hear their stories, not to tell your own. As an interviewer your job is to ask questions and listen, to ask probing follow up questions and to listen more. Probing follow up questions should be directed to the details of the story; for example, who did what, when, with whom, and with what results?

To Take Notes—or Not?

It is important to make note of the key stories, ideas and quotable quotes told to you during the interview. If you are able to take notes and listen attentively at the same time, then do so. If you find note taking to be distracting just jot down key words during the interview and take time afterwards to make notes.

Step 4: Whole-Team Data Sharing and Storytelling

After all of your team's interviews are done, get together to share and make meaning out of what you have learned. This will involve telling key stories to one another and sharing your interpretations of what those stories mean.

The minimum amount of time for data sharing is two hours, but it may take as long as four. The larger your team and the more interviews you have conducted, the more time you will need for data sharing and meaning making.

Begin the process by giving each team member a chance to share his or her data, without cross talk or discussion. Use your roles of discussion leader, timekeeper, and recorder to ensure that everybody stays on task and has relatively equal time.

You may have people share answers to each interview question, question by question. If you use this approach, have your recorder make notes of the key points on a flip chart as the stories are being told. Then after all the data and stories have been shared, as a group discuss and identify the key themes in three areas: 1) further dialogue needed, 2) decision required and 3) action needed.

Alternatively, you may find it easier to have individual interviewers do a preliminary synthesis of their data, reporting out to the whole team:

- What they found most surprising in their interviews.

- What they heard as the team's greatest strengths.

- The one most inspiring and compelling story they heard.

- The boldest vision they heard for the team's future.

Whatever approach you use be sure that all team members have ample time to share what they learned in their interviews.

Avoid the temptation to discuss ideas for actions and apparent changes; doing so will interrupt some of the long-term benefits of the storytelling and relationship-building process. Instead, record everybody's ideas on a flip chart and save them for later in the process.

Step 5: Mapping Your Team's Positive Core

Effective teams are strength based. They know their strengths and organize to optimize them. To move your team in this direction, it is useful to map your positive core—either in the way we've just described or using some other approach of your choosing.[11]

Begin by reflecting upon all the interview data and stories you shared. As a team, make a list of all the strengths, assets, resources and potentials of your team. Do not filter anything. Instead, be as comprehensive as possible in describing all the good traits of your team.

Once you have listed all of your team's most positive attributes, illustrate that positive core in a picture using a creative metaphor. For example, the leadership team of a small company symbolized its positive core as a baby elephant. This image conveyed compact, frisky and agile power: the team's ability to move faster than their larger competitors yet still have the resources and strengths to deliver solid service. Another team drew a picture of their "positive core pie," and wrote the recipe for their success based on their list of strengths, resources and assets.

The discussion and mapping of your team's positive core is an important step in enhancing your team's effectiveness. Take the time to listen to each team member's views about your team's strengths and to enjoy taking the time to affirm what you are doing well. Resist talking about all the things that are not going well. By keeping focused on your positive core, you will build the rapport and safety that will enable you to more easily discuss challenges and dissatisfactions at a later date. Building an appreciative foundation by mapping your positive core will support your team's short- and long-term success.

Step 6: Envisioning Your Team's Future

Now that you have discovered and discussed your team at its best and mapped its positive core, it is time to move your discussions into the future. You may do this by reviewing the data you collected about your team's future or by openly discussing your greatest hopes, dreams and wishes for the team. This is a time to be bold and creative, to imagine big possibilities, and to envision your dream team. It is also an important time to hear the personal hope, dreams and plans of each team member. By sharing personal dreams, you will begin to see how each member can better serve the team and be served by the team. So once again, go around and be sure that each team member has an opportunity for input into the discussion.

The best visions are specific and tangible as well as big and bold. Consider your ideal relationships within the team and with various stakeholders. Consider how you ideally would like to share information, make decisions, distribute work, determine the nature of leadership and planning and deal with resource allocation and finances among team members.

Use your positive core as inspiration for this process of envisioning. Imagine a team that is brimming with all the most positive qualities that you've discovered in Steps 3 through 5. Envision ways in which that positive core might be amplified and expanded even further, and seek out strategic opportunities that you have not yet capitalized upon.

Once you have seriously discussed and profiled your ideal future, do something creative to depict it as a team. Write a poem or song. Draw a picture. Act out "A Day in the Life of our Dream Team." This may seem like a silly or unnecessary activity, but we believe you will be positively surprised at the result. Taking time to be creative together and to practice "being the future you most desire" will contribute a great deal to your team's enthusiasm and energy for the future.

Step 7: Articulating Your Team's Purpose

Having created a bold and creative image of your team in the future, the next step is to turn this image into a concrete purpose statement. If you are simply revising an existing purpose statement, an hour may be enough time. If you are creating a team purpose statement for the first time, allow at least two hours and perhaps even longer.

A good purpose statement will tell you, your customers and your internal stakeholders why your team exists and/or what your team intends to accomplish. It will be simple and clear.

Consider the following sample team purpose statements:

> We on the *ABC* team assure our customers' success by anticipating business challenges with state-of-the-art IT solutions, quick turnaround and friendly, accessible service.

> We reinforce shareholder confidence and foster financial strength by providing wholly transparent, fully accessible reporting to all stakeholders, and by partnering with internal and external customers to develop and implement prudent, ethical and profitable financial practices that reinforce *XYZ*'s leadership of the international business community.

As you begin discussing your purpose as a team, be sure to connect back to the data and stories collected in your interviews. What does this information suggest about what is most valued and central to your team's being? What value do you add to your customers and stakeholders? What do team members hope to achieve together that they could not do alone?

At this point, it is a good idea to draft your purpose statement but not to finalize it. Instead, let it simmer while you create your team's guiding principles. You may even want to get input from some of your stakeholders before finalizing it.

Step 8: Crafting a Set of Guiding Principles for Your Team

High performance teams are conscious teams. They think about and decide together how they want to operate, treat one another and make decisions. And they hold themselves accountable to do as they say. Taking time to discuss and determine guiding principles is an investment in time that will pay off in the long run. Clear principles will foster high performance, collaboration and trust among team members.

Some of the areas around which you may want to craft principles include

- Communication

- Leadership

- Meeting management

- Decision-making

- Fun and happiness

- Pay and financial rewards

- Hiring

- Recognition

- Job assignment

- Membership and inclusion

- External partnerships

Fewer principles are better. Try to create the least number of principles as possible to truly guide your team to harmonious, high performance. The following team principles are examples for your consideration:

- Team information is transparent to all team members and stakeholders.

- When we are having fun we work. When we are not having fun we seek out and volunteer for other tasks.

- Hiring, performance reviews and salaries within the team are team decisions.

- We are all Chief Appreciation Officers.

The data and stories you collected during your interviews are valuable sources of information about how your team operates at its best. Review those again, along with your positive core map, to identify the most important three to five items for guiding principles. Identify and craft principles that will bring your dreams to life, as they are enacted on a daily basis.

Step 9: Clarifying Roles, Relationships and Responsibilities for Going Forward

Perhaps the best way to ensure commitment and enthusiasm for the team's work is to draw upon volunteer energy and self-responsibility. Clarification of ongoing roles, relationships and responsibilities must take place in the context of everything that you have discovered, discussed and dreamed so far in the process. Thus, team members should take time—first individually and then collectively—to reflect upon what they have learned and how it contributes to and is needed for the team's success.

Ask each team member to make a list of everything they will do more of, less of, and the same as on behalf of the team's success. Record those lists on separate pieces of flip chart paper and post them all on the wall.

As a team, walk around the room and read everyone's commitments. Ask questions to ensure understanding and discuss anything that needs to be clarified. Discuss the implications of these individual commitments on the team as a whole. What does the team wish to do more of, less of, and the same, as it moves forward into the future?

Make a master list of all of your individual and collective commitments, and distribute them to each team member for later reference.

It is also possible, following this collective choice making, that individual team members will need one-on-one discussions with others to clarify roles and responsibilities. If this is the case, schedule another time following the one-on-one discussions for the entire team to come back together and share the results of those side conversations.

Step 10: Celebrating Together

As we discussed in the introduction, high performance teams talk about themselves differently than not so successful teams. High performance teams are found to have a five to one ratio of positive to negative team talk.

In order to keep positive team talk alive and vibrant among your team members, organize regular team celebrations. Team celebrations may range from five minutes at the beginning of weekly staff meetings, talking about the best of the past week, to a quarterly review of performance high points, to a bulletin board displaying customer compliments, to an annual most valued team player award.

You want to do two things at this point in your team development process. One, discuss and plan for regular team celebrations. Determine what they will be, when they will occur and who will be responsible for making them happen.

Two, take time to acknowledge each other and share highlights from your positive team development process. Give each team member and the team as a whole a big pat on the back. Giving appreciative feedback to team members will boost your team spirit and help you to practice and develop your capacity to give appreciative feedback.

Sustaining Team High Performance through Appreciative Inquiry

Team development is a natural and ongoing process. Change is more the norm for most teams than routine. For high performance teams, change is an opportunity to tune into stakeholders and discover what they appreciate and need or want of the team. It is a chance to focus team activities upon those things that team members most value and want to achieve. And it is a time to renew and build relationships within the team and among team stakeholders. For high performance teams, change is an invitation for learning and development.

As a result, high performance teams keep learning and conscious development at the top of their agenda. They sustain their vitality and high performance through ongoing inquiry into what gives life to the team when it is at its best. We might even say, "An appreciative question a week helps a team stay at its peak."

Remember the two words: Appreciative Inquiry. Be an appreciative team by consciously focusing on the best in each other and in situations. Praise is the fuel of high performance. Be an inquiring team by regularly asking provocative questions, engaging in stimulating discussion, and trusting that vision, clarity, right relationship and right action will emerge in the process.

Section 5:
Building Your Own
Interview Guides

The blank interview guide on the following pages is a template for creating a customized, self-managed appreciative inquiry for your team (described in Section 3). Begin with the Initial Team Interview Guide, which introduces the process and begins the inquiry into teammates' best team experiences. Then proceed to the topic questions, which hone in on the specific areas most relevant to your team's needs. You'll also find an interview summary sheet to help you capture the most outstanding ideas and themes that emerge in each interview.

Interview Guide

Your Name: _____

Interviewee's Name: _____

Date: _____

Introduction:

Thank you for agreeing to share some of your valuable time in this team inquiry. Before we get started, I would like to explain more about what we hope to accomplish and how this process will work.

We want to make our team the very best it can be. Usually when people set out to reach their highest potential, they focus on identifying and solving problems so they can fix what is not working. We want to flip this strategy on its head and learn from our successes; we want to clarify the greatest strengths of our team and systematically expand our *positive core*. We want to mine all the insights and experiences that are already present within this team and apply them to making us even better than we already are.

This series of questions is set up to help us stay focused on our peak experiences, our times of great success—both here and on other teams. Maintaining this positive bias is not always easy since most of us have been trained to learn from our mistakes. Yet we may actually learn more from our triumphs. Immersing ourselves in memories of our achievements stirs up pride and boosts our energy. We become more open, eager to build on our most effective ways of working.

As we explore these questions, let's be conscious of staying on track with what works and discover how to make our best a more constant reality.

Any questions?

Opening:

Tell me about your beginnings with <u>this</u> team.

- What were your initial hopes, dreams and excitements as you first con-templated joining the group?

Now, describe a peak experience or high point in your experience with this team, a time when you felt most alive, most engaged, and proud of yourself, your co-workers and the work that you were doing.

- What were all the conditions and circumstances that contributed to that experience (e.g., you, other people, the task, the leadership, the process)

- How did your best qualities bring out the best in others and how did they inspire you to be the best you could possibly be?

Reflecting on this peak experience and other experiences of its kind, what do you most value about you and the unique skills, gifts, and talents that you bring to this team and the work that you do?

- What do you value most about this team and its larger mission in the organization—and in the world?

Topic Questions:

Enter the three to five questions (topic, lead-in and sub questions) your team has agreed to explore.

Closing:

It is one year from today. You have fallen into a magical sleep and suddenly, miraculously, everything that you have ever hoped or dreamed of for your team is true. You can truly say, without reservation, that this is the team of your dreams.

- Describe the team—its purpose, leadership, relationships, communication and processes. In general, describe how the work gets done and how it feels along the way.

What are you doing that is new or different? How does it feel to work in the team of your dreams?

If you could have any three wishes granted to immediately heighten the health and vitality of your existing team, what would they be?

As you reflect back on this interview experience, what is the most important thing you have learned (or perhaps learned again) about yourself, your team, and the organization of which you are a part?

Section 6:
Conclusion

Imagine what a harmonious world it could be if every single person,
both young and old, shared a little of what he is good at doing.

—Quincy Jones

This book is a call to action. It is a bold invitation to transform your team through the power of positive questions. While reading it may trigger new perspectives, its potential can only be realized through use. Nurturing your team on positive questions can appreciatively impact every aspect of team life. It can fortify your team's identity, roles, relationships and leadership as well as processes for decision-making, communication and recognition.

The 48 questions in this book give you opportunities to get to know the other members of your team, talk about those things that are most significant to your team's well being and success and explore your team's positive core. When a team has conscious knowledge of its positive core, it is better able to develop and apply its inherent talents and optimize its resources. It is more capable of aligning strengths and making weaknesses irrelevant. Collaborative inquiry, dialogue, and appreciative exploration nurture a team's strengths. They uplift people's spirit and energy, and stimulate team success.

Adapt this book to your team's unique needs, dreams and state of development. Each team forms and develops in unique ways; thus, different teams will benefit from different questions in this book. For example, early in a team's life people need to get to know one another. They need to clarify and agree to their purpose as well as their reasons for being on the team. They need to discover the strengths and resources that each member brings to the table. As teams develop over time, however, they need to pay more attention to role clarity, communication and decision making processes. They need to acknowledge and optimize differences by learning about and valuing people's unique opinions, approaches, styles and ideas. And of course, as they begin to achieve great results, it is the rewards, recognitions and celebrations that keep the team's spirit and energy high. Whatever your team's unique developmental stage or challenge, there are questions in this book that will help you move forward via meeting starters, team meetings, or conscious and deliberate team development processes.

This book suggests a positive approach to team development. It is based on the principles and practices of Appreciative Inquiry.[12] So we start with a deceptively simple premise: develop your team by discovering and expanding what already works. For many this positive bias is a new way to look at teams. We might even say that it provides new eyes for an ongoing journey toward high performance.

The positive bias of the questions in this book represents a clear shift in worldview—from deficits to strengths, from problems to possibilities, from criticism to appreciation, from shame and fear to pride and compassion. Driven by the rewards of this fundamental shift in how we work and live together, a positive revolution is gaining momentum. To learn more, refer to our closing sections. There you will find everything from websites to work-shops to facilitators to speakers—all related to positive approaches to organizational change and team development and all helping you to learn how to apply Appreciative Inquiry within your organization.

We believe that this book will help you to bring out the best of your team. We hope, at a minimum, that it will stimulate dialogue about the things you and your colleagues most care about and believe to be central to your team's ongoing success. Taking time to talk openly using a structured format and ensuring that everyone has a chance to talk and to be heard will build team identity and cohesion. The more people can speak about what is in their hearts and on their minds, the more they will want to be part of the listening team, organization or community. Keep conversations affirmative by focusing on what gives life and vitality to team members, and you will create a sense of safety and loyalty within the team. The more people are asked to talk about their strengths, both individually and collectively, the more they will draw upon those strengths and optimize them in the service of the whole.

Recently, we asked participants in an Appreciative Inquiry-based, team-building process to describe their experience. Their descriptions were effusive:

- *We got so much done and no one was blamed, criticized or told what to do.*

- *This was surprisingly fun and very productive.*

- *We need to do this more often. It was so easy to focus on the positive, once we got over our habits of focusing on the problems. Now we have new habits that will truly let us soar together.*

We anticipate that you and your teammates will have similar experiences as you work with the resources we have provided for self-managed team development. We trust that this book will continually enhance your ability to bring out the best in your team, and to help people envision positive possibilities for the future. We hope that each time you use the questions in this book, they become more and more your own—until the day when you will approach everything you do with positive questions. When this happens, you and your colleagues will enjoy your work and your lives even more fully. You will be drawn to one another and to high performance. People, relationships and teams thrive when viewed through appreciative eyes.

Endnotes

[1] Whitney, D. and Trosten-Bloom, A. *The Power of Appreciative Inquiry*. San Francisco: Berrett-Koehler, 2003.

[2] Bion,W. R. *Experiences In Groups*. New York: Ballantine Books, 1961.

[3] Smith, K. and Berg, D. *Paradoxes Of Group Life*. San Francisco: Jossey-Bass, 1987.

[4] Losade, M. and Heaphy, E. "The Role of Positivity and Connectivity in Performance of Business Teams: A Nonlinear Dynamic Model," in *American Behavioral Scientist*, Vol. 47, No. 6, 2004, pp. 740–765.

[5] Fredrickson, B. L. "What Good Are Positive Emotions?" in *Review of General Psychology*, Vol. 2, No. 3, 1998, pp. 300–319.

[6] R. Rubin, I. and Plovnick, M., 1981, "Dynamics of Groups that Execute or Manage Policy," in Payne, R. & Cooper, C. (Eds.), *Groups at Work*. New York: John Wiley & Sons, 1981.

[7] Katzenbach, J. R. and Smith, D. K. *The Wisdom of Teams*. New York: Harper Collins, 1993.

[8] Bushe, G. R. "Meaning Making in Teams: Appreciative Inquiry with Pre-identity and Postidentity Teams," in Fry, R., Barrett, F, Seiling, J. & Whitney D. (Eds.) *Appreciative Inquiry and Organizational Transformation: Reports from the Field*. Westport: Quorum, 2002.

[9] Bushe, G. R. and Coetzer, G. "Appreciative Inquiry as a Team Development Intervention" in *Journal of Applied Behavioral Science*, Vol. 31, No. 1, 1995, pp. 19–30.

[10] For additional tips on conducting appreciative interviews, see Whitney, D. and Trosten-Bloom, A., *The Power of Appreciative Inquiry*, pp. 162–164.

[11] Ibid., p. 168.

[12] Ibid., pp. 1–4.

About the Authors

Diana Whitney, Ph.D. is President of Corporation for Positive Change, a Founder of the Taos Institute and Distinguished Consulting Faculty at Saybrook Graduate School and Research Center. An internationally recognized consultant, keynote speaker, and thought leader on the subjects of Appreciative Inquiry, positive change and spirituality at work, she has taught at Antioch University, Case Western Reserve University, Ashridge Management Institute (UK) and Eisher Institute (India). Diana is also an award winning author and editor of dozens of books and articles on positive approaches to change. A premier consultant in the area of large-scale change, her clients include: Ameriquest Mortgage Company; British Airways; First Caribbean International Bank; Hunter Douglas Window Fashions; GTE-Verizon; Johnson & Johnson; NY Power Authority; Sandia National Labs; the United Religions Initiative; and Waggener Edstrom. Along with teaching and consulting, Diana is a spiritual counselor, artist and healer. She lives in Taos, NM and can be reached at diana@positivechange.org or www.positivechange.org.

Amanda Trosten-Bloom is a Principal with Corporation for Positive Change. A nationally acclaimed consultant, trainer and author in the field of Appreciative Inquiry, Amanda's work focuses primarily on facilitating strength-based whole-system change in the areas of culture transformation, strategic planning, mergers and acquisitions, leadership development and business process improvement. Over the course of 25 years as a consultant and manager, she has worked in a variety of arenas including manufacturing, service, high-tech, education, health care, financial and scientific. Her clients include: Accenture Consulting; Ameriquest Mortgage Company; Front Range Community College; Hunter Douglas North America; McDATA Corporation; the National

Security Administration; Regis University; and the United Religions Initiative. Amanda lives near Denver, CO and can be reached at amanda@ positivechange.org or www.positivechange.org.

Jay K. Cherney, Ph.D. is a psychologist, consultant, mediator, speaker and performer. He brings a wealth of clinical experience to the work of facilitating collaborative relationships in teams and organizations, and helps clients construct more useful conversations. His keynote speech on "Resilient Thinking" proposes that we reach our highest potential in today's complexity when we play with multiple meanings and stories. A co-owner of Appreciative Inquiry Consulting, Jay has worked with healthcare and pharmaceutical clients, including several Johnson & Johnson companies. He is also a mediator for the US Postal Service. Jay lives near Philadelphia, PA and can be reached at jcherney@aiconsulting.org, jcherney@netreach.net or www. appreciativeteambuilding.com.

Ronald Fry, Ph.D. is an Associate Professor of Organizational Behavior and Faculty Director of the Executive MBA Program at Case Western Reserve University, Weatherhead School of Management. A co-originator of the Appreciative Inquiry philosophy and practice, Ron has conducted Appreciative Leadership and Organization Capacity Building programs in more than 30 countries. He recently co-edited the first case book on Appreciative Inquiry, *Appreciative Inquiry and Organizational Transformation: Reports from the Field.* His clients include: Roadway Express; World Vision Relief; and the US Navy. Ron lives in Cleveland, OH and can be reached at rxf5@po.cwru.ed or www.weatherhead.cwru.edu.

Additional Books
by the Authors

The Power of Appreciative Inquiry: A Practical Guide to Positive Change, Berrett Koehler Publishers, 2002

The Encyclopedia of Positive Questions: Using Appreciative Inquiry to Bring Out the Best of Your Organization, Lakeshore Communications, 2002

Appreciative Inquiry and Organizational Transformation: Reports from the Field, Quorum Books, 2002

The Appreciative Inquiry Handbook, Lakeshore Communications, 2003

The Appreciative Inquiry Summit: A Practitioner's Guide for Leading Large Group Change, Berrett Koehler Publishers, 2003

Positive Approaches to Peacebuilding, PACT Publications, 2003

Appreciative Inquiry Resources

Team Development Consulting and Workshops

Corporation for Positive Change www.positivechange.org
>An international consulting firm focused on AI and the practice of positive change in business, not for profit, educational, religious and governmental organizations.

Taos Institute www.taosinstitute.net
>An international community focused upon the advancement of social constructionist theory and practice in organizations, families and communities.

Appreciative Teambuilding www.appreciativeteambuilding.com
>A consulting firm specializing in AI and team building.

Appreciative Inquiry Consulting www.aiconsulting.org
>An international network of AI practitioners who collaborate for learning, hosting conferences and delivering AI training and consulting.

Appreciative Inquiry Related Websites and Listserve

Appreciative Inquiry Commons www.appreciativeinquiry.cwru.edu/
>   An open source website with information, samples and case studies about AI.

AI Practitioner www.**aipractitioner**.com
>   A monthly electronic newsletter with articles about AI in practice.

AI Listserv ailist@lists.business.utah.edu
>   An ongoing dialogue among AI practitioners around the world.

0-595-33503-9

Printed in the United States
67728LVS00003B/142-174